CONVERSATIONS

Getting to Know the Ones You Love

KENNY ROCHON, III
& DR. SMILEY

Conversations

ISBN: 978-1-64810-326-1

Published by Perfect Publishing, Co.

Printed in the United States of America

When you were young what did you want to be when you grew up?

What is your biggest accomplishment?

What is your favorite place in America?

Have you ever had an experience that led you to believe in angels or ghosts?

What animal would you want to be and why?

If you could be anyone, who would you be? How about if you could be anyone for 30 days... what would you do?

Would you rather be a celebrity and have many assaults against you and be rich and famous or live in a quiet world with no chasers and no dangerous people?

If you could work as an assistant to anyone for a year, who would you choose?

If you could be a famous athlete for a single game, who would you be?

Has anything bad ever happened to you that turned out to be for the best?

Have you ever been Bullied?

What kind of business would you love to start?

What book changed your life? And if you could only keep one of your books, which would you keep and why?

If you were to own a fabulously impractical car what car would it be?

How was your childhood?

Which is more important common sense or intelligence?

Where would you choose to live if you had to leave this country?

Is it more essential to develop beliefs or gain knowledge?

Would you die for your country? And how do you feel about people who die for their country?

If you could be a cat or dog and why?

What celebrity do people say you resemble?

Do you believe in coincidence or synchronicity?

If you had to spend one year living alone in a remote cabin, what would you spend your time doing?

What do you complain about more than anything else?

Where would you choose to live if you had to leave this country?

If you could do something dangerous just once with no risk what would you do?

What are your favorite Disney experience?

If you could only read one book genre for the rest of your life, what would it be?

What would you most like to do for someone else if you had the money and time?

What are your favorite 3 life experiences so far? And what life experience has strengthened you the most?

Would you rather be famous or wealthy?

What is your greatest fear?

What one fear would you like to conquer?

Have you ever been in a fight?

Is forgiveness or justice more important?

What are the most important qualities you look for in friends?

What is one goal you hope to accomplish this year?

What would you most like to ask God?

Would you rather meet a great, great, grandparents or your great, great, grandchildren?

What's the hardest thing you've ever done?

Would you rather be healthy or wealthy?

How do you define 'Hero' and who is your hero?

What historical time period would you most like to visit?

If you could master one instrument which, would it be?

Would you rather eat dairy or vegetables for the rest of your life?

Would you stop eating all junk food to live five years longer?

What is your favorite joke?

Which language would you like to speak fluently?

What makes you laugh the hardest?

Would you like a quiet life of safety or a life of great adventure and uncertainty?

If you could bring anyone back to life, who would it be?

Do you live more in the past, present or future?

Would you rather live by the beach or in the mountains?

If you only had five more years to live, would you change anything about your life?

If you lived to be 100, would it be more important to have a sharp mind or a fit body?

If you could change one thing about the way you look, what would it be?

What was your favorite childhood meal?

If you didn't have to worry about money, what would you do with your life?

If you could make a movie, what would it be about?

What is your favorite movie?

What movie inspires you the most?

If you could have another name, what would you choose?

What is the nicest thing you have ever done?

What do you wish you were better at saying 'No" to?

What obligation do you believe you have to your country?

At what age do most people become old and what is the secret to staying young?

Which of your personality traits would you most like to change?

What is your purpose in life?

Which piece of land would you wish to have preserved forever?

Would you rather be rich or smart?

What is your favorite song?

Who do you think is the most important person alive today?

What's the most beautiful place you've ever seen?

Which is more important the respect of your children or your parents?

If you were offered a seat on the next space shuttle, would you take it?

Have you ever swum with sharks or any other marine life?

What has been the most spiritual experience of your life?

If you could have one superpower, what would it be and what would you do with it?

Would you choose to be the worst player on a winning team or the best player on a losing team?

What did you get into the most trouble for when you were young?

What remains undone that you've wanted to get done for years?

What's the most significant problem in the world?

Is it more difficult for you to speak kindly or honestly?

Would you be likely to survive alone in the wilderness?

If you got a temporary tattoo, what would it be and what would it mean?

What is the most amazing weather you've seen and what is the best way to spend a rainy weekend?

In your opinion what are the seven wonders of the world?

Which temptation do you try the hardest to resist?

If you could give all human beings one virtue which would you choose?

What would you love to find at a yard sale?

Would you rather live in high cold or hot?

Would you rather have an allergy to peanut or high cold weathers?

What is the most dangerous thing that was fun for you?

Would you rather be a musician or magician?

Would you rather be able to stop time or read minds?

How would you like to spend your elder years?

Would you move to space or stay at earth?

Would you rather be respected or have money?

Would you rather have everyone accept you and think you are amazing and know you are not. Or would you rather be

amazing, and no one knows it?

Would you rather be skinny and strong or buff but weak?

Would you rather eat only meat and be super fat and unhealthy or you could only eat vegetables and you would be super powerful and healthy?

BONUS

Would you rate this book five of five on amazon or lower?

Would you rather rate this book on amazon or be lazy?

More Books From

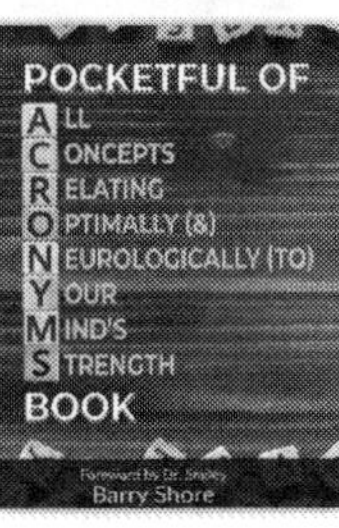

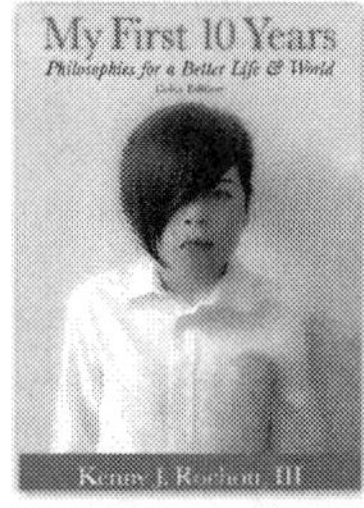

www.PerfectPublishing.com

More Books From

PerfectPublishing.com

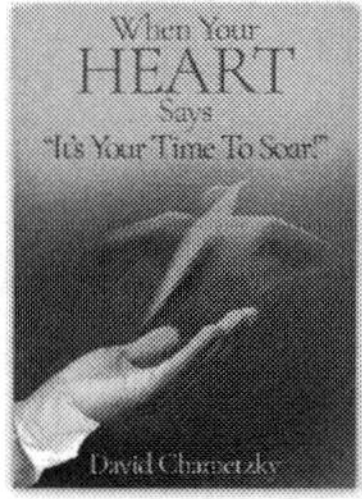

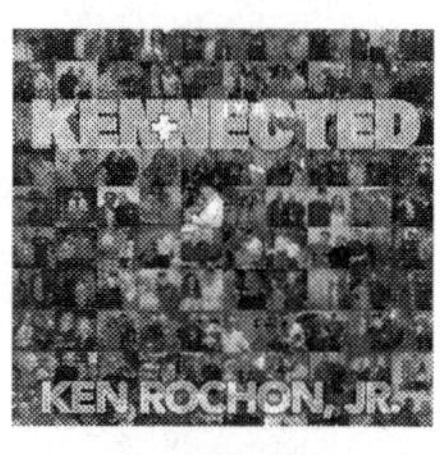

www.PerfectPublishing.com